A Note to Parents

Eyewitness Readers is a compelling new program for beginning readers, designed in conjunction with leading literacy experts, including Dr. Linda Gambrell, President of the National Reading Conference and past board member of the International Reading Association.

Eyewitness has become the most trusted name in illustrated books, and this new series combines the highly visual *Eyewitness* approach with engaging, easy-to-read stories. Each *Eyewitness Reader* is guaranteed to capture a child's interest while developing his or her reading skills, general knowledge, and love of reading.

The four levels of *Eyewitness Readers* are aimed at different reading abilities, enabling you to choose the books that are exactly right for your children:

Level 1, for **Preschool to Grade 1**
Level 2, for **Grades 1 to 3**
Level 3, for **Grades 2 and 3**
Level 4, for **Grades 2 to 4**

The "normal" age at which a child begins to read can be anywhere from three to eight years old, so these levels are intended only as a general guideline.

No matter which level you select, you can be sure that you are helping your child learn to read, then read to learn!

A DK PUBLISHING BOOK
www.dk.com

Editor Dawn Sirett
Art Editor Jane Horne

Senior Editor Linda Esposito
Senior Art Editor Diane Thistlethwaite
US Editor Regina Kahney
Production Melanie Dowland
Picture Researcher Cynthia Frazer
Jacket Designer Karen Lieberman
Natural History Consultant
Theresa Greenaway

Reading Consultant
Linda B. Gambrell, Ph.D.

First American Edition, 2000
2 4 6 8 10 9 7 5 3 1
Published in the United States by DK Publishing, Inc.
95 Madison Avenue, New York, New York 10016

Published in Great Britain by Dorling Kindersley Limited.

Eyewitness Readers™ is a trademark of Dorling Kindersley Limited, London.

Library of Congress Cataloging-in-Publication Data

Moses, Brian.
   Winking, blinking, wiggling, and waggling / by Brian Moses.-- 1st American ed.
      p. cm. -- (Eyewitness readers)
   Summary: Describes different eyes and ears in the animal kingdom
and how they are used.
   ISBN 0-7894-5414-9 (hc) -- ISBN 0-7894-5413-0 (pb)
   1. Eye--Juvenile literature. 2. Ear--Juvenile literature. [1. Eye. 2. Ear. 3.
Animals.] I. Title. II. Series.

QL949.S57 2000
573.8'8--dc21   99-044161

Color reproduction by Colourscan, Singapore
Printed and bound in Belgium by Proost

The publisher would like to thank the following for
their kind permission to reproduce their photographs:
Key: a=above, c=center, b=below, l=left, r=right, t=top
Ardea London Ltd: Kenneth W. Fink 10 br, 26 br, M. Watson 32 br;
Biofotos: C. Andrew Henley 11 tr; **Bruce Coleman Collection Ltd**: Alain
Compost 13 b, Chrisler Fredriksson 31 b, Johnny Johnson 25 br, Kim Taylor
32 cr; **Sylvia Cordaiy Photo Library Ltd**: Colin Hoskins 18–19 b; **Julian
Cotton Photo Library**: front cover br; **Oxford Scientific Films**: David Cayless
27 t, Tim Jackson 18 tl, Steve Littlewood 16 c, Frank Schneidermeyer 23 br,
Ian West 15 br; **Premaphotos Wildlife**: Ken Preston-Mafham 10 acl;
Tony Stone Images: front cover background; ©**Jerry Young**: 30 c.

Additional credits:
Peter Anderson, Geoff Brightling, Jane Burton, Geoff Dann, Mike Dunning, Neil
Fletcher, Steve Gorton, Frank Greenaway, Dave King, Cyril Laubscher, Will Long
and Richard Davies – Oxford Scientific Films, Tracy Morgan, Kim Taylor, and
Jerry Young (additional photography for DK); Lynn Bresler (for the index).

DK EYEWITNESS READERS

Level 2
GRADES 1-3

Winking, Blinking,
Wiggling, and Waggling

Written by Brian Moses

DK PUBLISHING, INC.

Eyes are for looking,
seeing, and staring.

Eyes are for watching,
gazing, and glaring.

Eyes are for squinting, winking, and blinking.

Eyes are for prying, spying, and spotting.

Eyes are for peeking, peeping, and sleeping ... zzzzzz!

Whose eyes are these?

He sleeps by day
and hunts by night.
His loud "hoo hoo"
gives mice a fright.

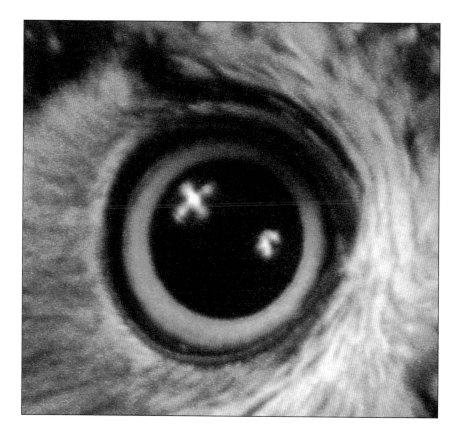

This sea creature is
cleverer than you think.
He hides from enemies
by firing black ink.

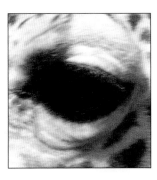

He stretches his neck
to the top of a tree
and eats all the leaves
that he can see.

She lies very still.
She could be asleep.
But if birds come close
just watch her leap!

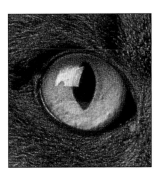

Were you right? Turn the page ...

Some animals see
much better
than we do.

An owl's huge eyes
help him
to hunt for food
in low light.

A squid needs to see
in deep, dark water.

Giraffes have very good eyesight and can see long distances.

A cat sees about six times as well as we do at night.

Cats' eyes

A cat's eyes shine at night because mirror-like parts in them reflect light. Many animals have mirror-like parts in their eyes to help them see in low light.

Mom says, "I haven't got eyes
in the back of my head."

But a jumping spider
has eight eyes
all around her head.

She has two large eyes
that look forward.
Her other six eyes are smaller
and look to her back and sides.

Four eyes

Four-eyed fish live near the
surface of water. Their eyes
are divided in two so they can
see enemies in the air and
in the water at the same time!

A horsefly can see
in every direction
because a fly's eyes are made up
of hundreds of tiny parts.
Eyes like this are called
compound eyes.

This is why it is so hard to swat a fly.
He can see you coming
from every direction!

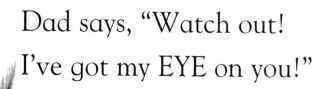

Dad says, "Watch out!
I've got my EYE on you!"

But if a vulture has his eye
on a sick animal,
it had better watch out.
Vultures feed on dead animals and
can spot a sick animal far away.
Birds of prey like vultures
have the keenest eyesight of all birds.

Tarsiers wake up at night.
Their large eyes
help them to spot danger
in the rainforest after dark.

They can also turn their heads
almost full circle
to keep a lookout for enemies.

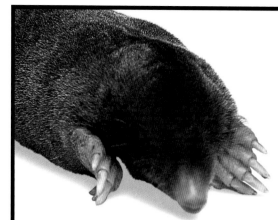

Mom says,
"Watch where
you're going!"

But a mole has tiny eyes and
can't really see where he's going.

Moles spend most of their time
digging underground,
so they don't need big eyes.

Earthworms have no eyes at all!
They live underground.

If they come above ground,
their other senses tell them
if there is movement nearby.
Then they hide quickly
in case an enemy is coming.

Larder for later
Moles find worms to eat
by smelling and touching.
Sometimes they store
the worms in a mole larder
and eat them later.

Dad says, "Don't throw things!
You'll knock someone's eye out!"

But snails don't have to worry
about their eyes.

Snails have their eyes
on the ends of long stalks.
If a snail senses danger,
he pulls the stalks inside his head.

An extra eyelid
Birds of prey, such as
this eagle, have a
layer of clear skin
that flicks over their eye
to clean and protect it.

A camel's eyes are protected, too.
She has two rows of eyelashes
to keep out the desert sand
and the glare of the sun.

Ears are for hearing,
harking, and heeding.

Ears are for listening,
snooping, and sneaking.

Ears are for washing,
wiggling, and waggling.

Ears are for pricking up,
picking up, and tuning-in.

Ears are for
flapping ...

but not
for flying!

Whose ears are these?

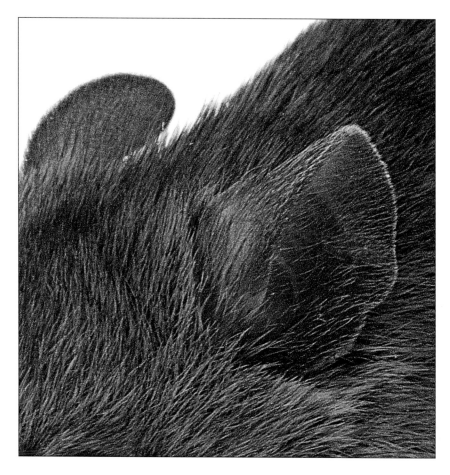

She has a long, furry tail
and dainty feet.
At night she goes looking
for something to eat.

He lives in a burrow
under the ground.
He hops away
if he hears a sound.

She's a bit like a monkey.
She's a bit like a bear.
She's a bit like a baby
with her wide-eyed stare.

He's orange and black
and hunts at night.
His open mouth
is a scary sight.

Were you right? Turn the page …

Many animals can hear
much better than we can.

A mouse has large ears
so she can sense
danger nearby.

A rabbit can hear
when an enemy
is creeping up
behind him.

A bushbaby's ears
help her to hear
the insects
she hunts at night.

A tiger hunts at dusk
or at night
and can hear
small animals
rustling in the grass.

Keep an eye on the ears
Tigers have white spots
on the backs of their ears.
People think that these
help cubs to keep track
of their mothers in dense jungle.

Mom says, "Don't mumble.
I can't hear a word you're saying."

But many animals can hear sounds
that are outside our hearing range.

We can't hear the high sound
of a dog whistle.
But a dog can.

Bats catch insects
by making
high squeaks
that we can't hear.

Their squeaks bounce off
insects and come back as echoes.
A bat can then figure out
how far away an insect is.

Whale talk

Whales talk by making
sounds called songs. We can't
hear them from far away, but
whales hear each other call
from hundreds of miles away.

Dad says, "Can you wiggle
your ears?"

Not many
people can.

But foxes can wiggle their ears.
They turn them to hear
where a sound is coming from.

Worm alert!
A fox's hearing is so good
that he can catch worms
by listening for the rustling
of their bristles on the grass.

Rhinos also turn their large ears
to pick up sounds.

Kangaroos do this, too.
They can turn
their ears
in the exact direction
of a noise.

Mom says,
"Listen when I'm talking to you.
You've got ears, haven't you?"

But some creatures
don't seem to have ears at all.

Birds' ears are two small holes
in the sides of their heads,
which are covered
by feathers.

Fish have ears inside their skulls.

Snakes don't have
outer ears.
They are deaf
to most sounds,
but they can
pick up footsteps
and other vibrations
from the ground.

Frog ears

Frogs and toads
have large flat eardrums
just behind their eyes.
They need good hearing
to listen out for enemies.

Dad says, "I'm all ears."
But some animals really are!

A fennec fox hears
the tiniest sound
with his huge ears.
Air blowing over his ears
also cools his blood,
which keeps him cool in the desert.

Each of an African elephant's ears can be 5 ¹/₂ feet (1.7 meters) across! She flaps her ears to cool down.

Animals with such amazing ears never forget to wash behind them ... even if you forget to wash behind yours!

More Fascinating Facts

Starfish have a very simple type of eye on the tip of each arm.

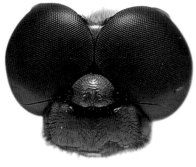

Dragonflies have the biggest eyes of any insect. They have up to 40,000 lenses in each eye.

A chameleon is able to look in two directions at once.

The 56-foot (17-meter) giant squid has the biggest eyes of any creature. They can be up to 16 inches (40 centimeters) wide.

A fox lays her ears flat if she isn't going to attack. When her ears are up, she is ready to pounce.

When swimming, crocodiles are able to close their ears to keep out water.

A camel's ears are lined with fur to keep out blowing sand.

A grasshopper's ears are under his wings.